TABLE OF CONTENTS

Introduction

ONE ISLAND, TWO WORLDS

A door clanged. **Inmates** shuffled into their cells. Guards scowled. Just a quarter mile away, the sound of laughter drifted into the air. Kids zoomed by on skates. Boys headed down to the water to fish. Girls balanced on an old cannon, giggling. On Alcatraz, life in the toughest prison in the country was grim. For the guards and their families who lived on the island, it was just home.

In the 1800s and early 1900s, the tiny island of Alcatraz in San Francisco Bay housed a fort and a military prison. The families of the men who worked there called Alcatraz home.

In 1934, the island entered its most famous era. For the next 29 years, Alcatraz was known as "the Rock." It was a maximum-security prison for inmates who were considered escape risks. Mobsters Al Capone and Mickey Cohen were just two of the **notorious** criminals who lived there. Because of its high security, Alcatraz needed many staff members to run the prison.

ISLAND LIFE

In 1933, the 17-year-old daughter of a military man stationed on Alcatraz swam about a mile to San Francisco. She was the first female on record to make the dangerous crossing.

Teen girls pose on one of the many abandoned cannons on Alcatraz.

Some of these employees lived in San Francisco and **commuted** daily by boat. Many others lived on the island with their families. It wasn't just more convenient. The apartments on Alcatraz were cheaper than those in the expensive city of San Francisco. As a result, dozens of children lived on Alcatraz. They grew up within shouting distance of some of the toughest criminals in the country.

Living on Alcatraz had its drawbacks. There were many rules. Getting to the mainland was a challenge. Cold winds whipped the island in winter. And in summer, thick fog often covered everything, accompanied by window-rattling fog horns.

Despite the downsides, the children who grew up on Alcatraz later reported that it was a huge privilege and pleasure. Their childhood was unlike that of any other children in the country. Living so close together, they were almost like an enormous family.

Chapter 1

A MINI CITY ON THE ROCK

For the kids living on Alcatraz, the island was like a friendly village. Everyone knew each other. A little grocery store sold the basics. It had fresh produce, canned goods, bread, cereal, and a small selection of meat.

There were no cell phones back then. Instead, apartments had land lines. But residents could only use them to call other people on the island.

Building 64 was where most of the guards' families lived.

Calling someone off the island was more complicated. In the early days, everyone shared one public pay phone that they had to insert a coin into before dialing the number. Receiving a call required setting a time beforehand for someone to call. Then a person would wait by the phone until it rang. One woman remembered the guards teasing her when she was a teenager every time she took a call from her boyfriend in San Francisco.

Most of the children's fathers were prison guards. One guard's wife volunteered as the postmistress. She sorted the incoming mail for the families and inmates. A guard screened every inmate letter.

For certain jobs, such as laundry, inmates worked for the employees. Once a week, inmates went into kids' homes to pick up dirty laundry. Inmates cleaned and dried the items in the prison and delivered them back to the families.

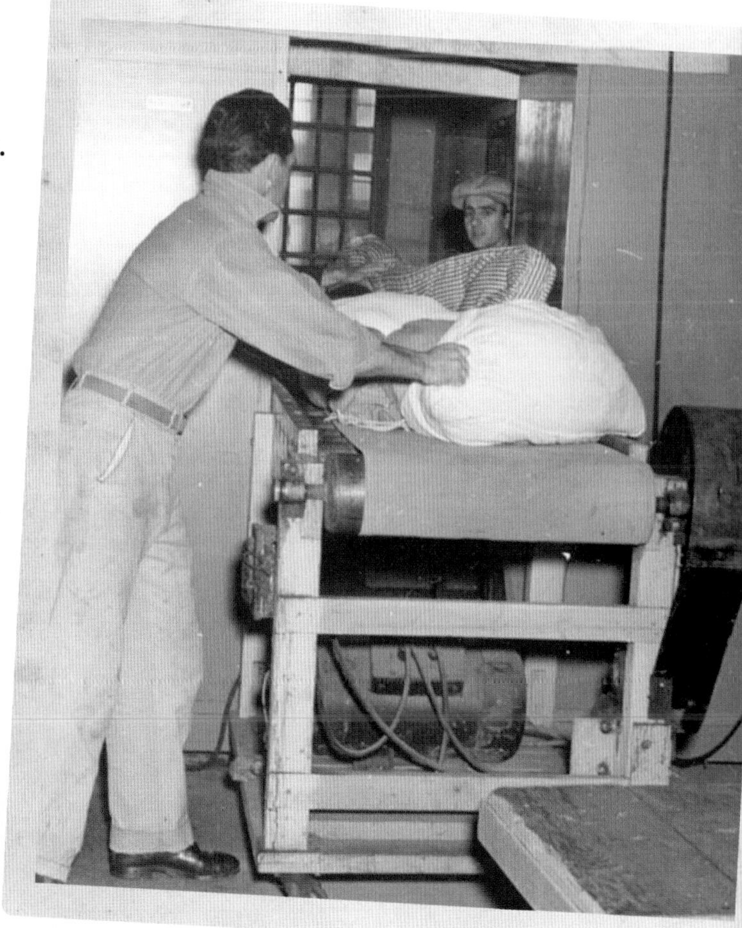

Inmates sent laundry through a metal detector when they brought it back to the prison. That way, weapons could not be snuck in.

The homes for kids on Alcatraz were like homes anywhere else. A few families were assigned a cottage. The majority, though, lived in apartments, contained in several concrete apartment blocks. These buildings were grouped on one side of the island, away from the inmates but within view of them.

The apartments were simple. But many of the kids who lived there liked them. The living arrangements made it easy for them to simply step outside to play with their friends!

When it wasn't foggy, children took in a breathtaking view of the San Francisco skyline! The residents of the island even had a front-row seat to the construction of the Golden Gate Bridge and the San Francisco-Oakland Bay Bridge.

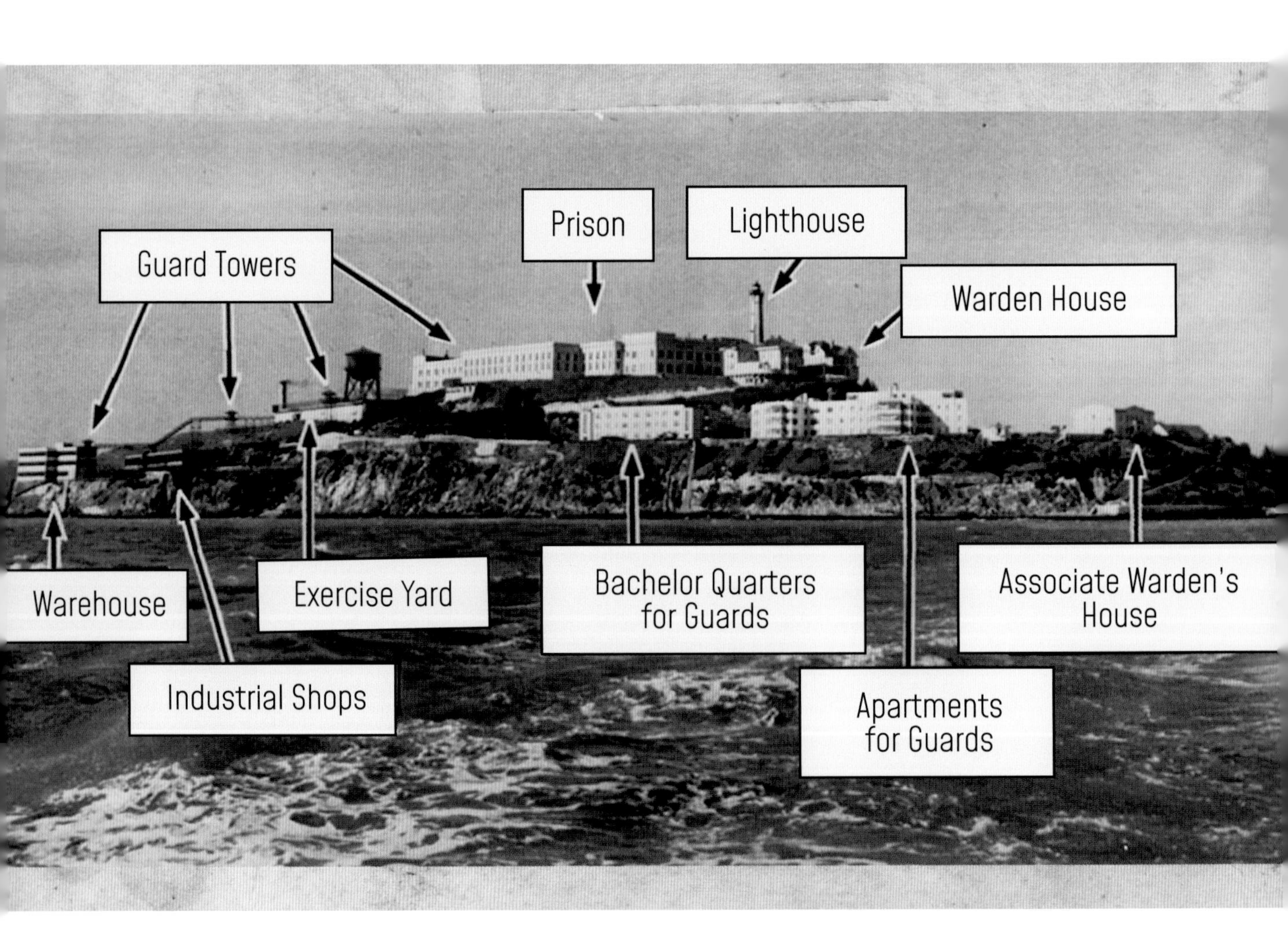

Inmates had the same view, but most looked on it differently. Seeing the city across the bay, so close and yet out of reach, was a constant reminder of what they were missing out on because of their crimes.

The Golden Gate Bridge, 1933

Jobs on Alcatraz

Most of the employees on Alcatraz were guards. There were also wardens, mechanics, electricians, boat operators, medical professionals, cooks, and lighthouse keepers.

Inmates were required to perform jobs too. They worked under guard supervision. Some worked in laundry and shoe repair or in the shop making uniforms, gloves, or furniture. Others loaded and unloaded boats on the docks or did handyman or sanitation work. Kitchen and garden duty were two of the most popular inmate jobs.

Chapter 2

SAFETY FIRST

Hundreds of the most dangerous people in America lived under one roof on one small island. Most dreamed of escaping. A few even did—although they probably died crossing the bay. It must have been a scary place for the families, right?

Nope! The families on Alcatraz figured it was safer than anywhere else. After all, guards were always on watch. Other prisons employed about one guard per every 12 inmates. On Alcatraz, there was one for every three inmates!

Train cars holding Alcatraz's first prisoners were floated across the bay on barges.

There were no cars and few worries of crime. Most people never even locked their doors. Security was so tight that when the first inmates arrived in the San Francisco Bay Area by train, the train cars were loaded right onto barges. The prisoners crossed the water to Alcatraz still inside the train cars, so they had no chance of escape.

There were many rules to keep the children safe. Kids were not allowed inside the prison. They also weren't supposed to wander outside of approved areas—but most kids broke this rule now and then.

The biggest rule? No interacting with the inmates! This was another rule that got broken occasionally. One former resident remembered passing a candy bar to an inmate on a work crew. The inmate told the boy to do well in school so he wouldn't end up in prison like him. Another boy accidentally dropped a toy from a balcony. He called down to an inmate on the dock. The inmate helped him get the toy back with a fishing line.

The real dangers on Alcatraz were natural ones—the steep cliffs and dangerous water. San Francisco Bay had strong tides and currents—and maybe even sharks. Parents worried when their kids fished off the dock, but luckily, no one ever fell in.

Kids on Alcatraz were accustomed to playing near fences and barbed war.

Meeting Mr. Capone

Everyone wanted to know about the really famous criminals, like Chicago crime boss Al Capone. One boy actually met Capone and shook his hand. The boy was having an asthma attack, so his father took him to the prison clinic. Al Capone was there, mopping the floor. Another child remembers that after she sent her shoes to the prison for repair, they came back all fixed up—and with Capone's name signed on their soles! She later greatly regretted throwing away the shoes when she outgrew them.

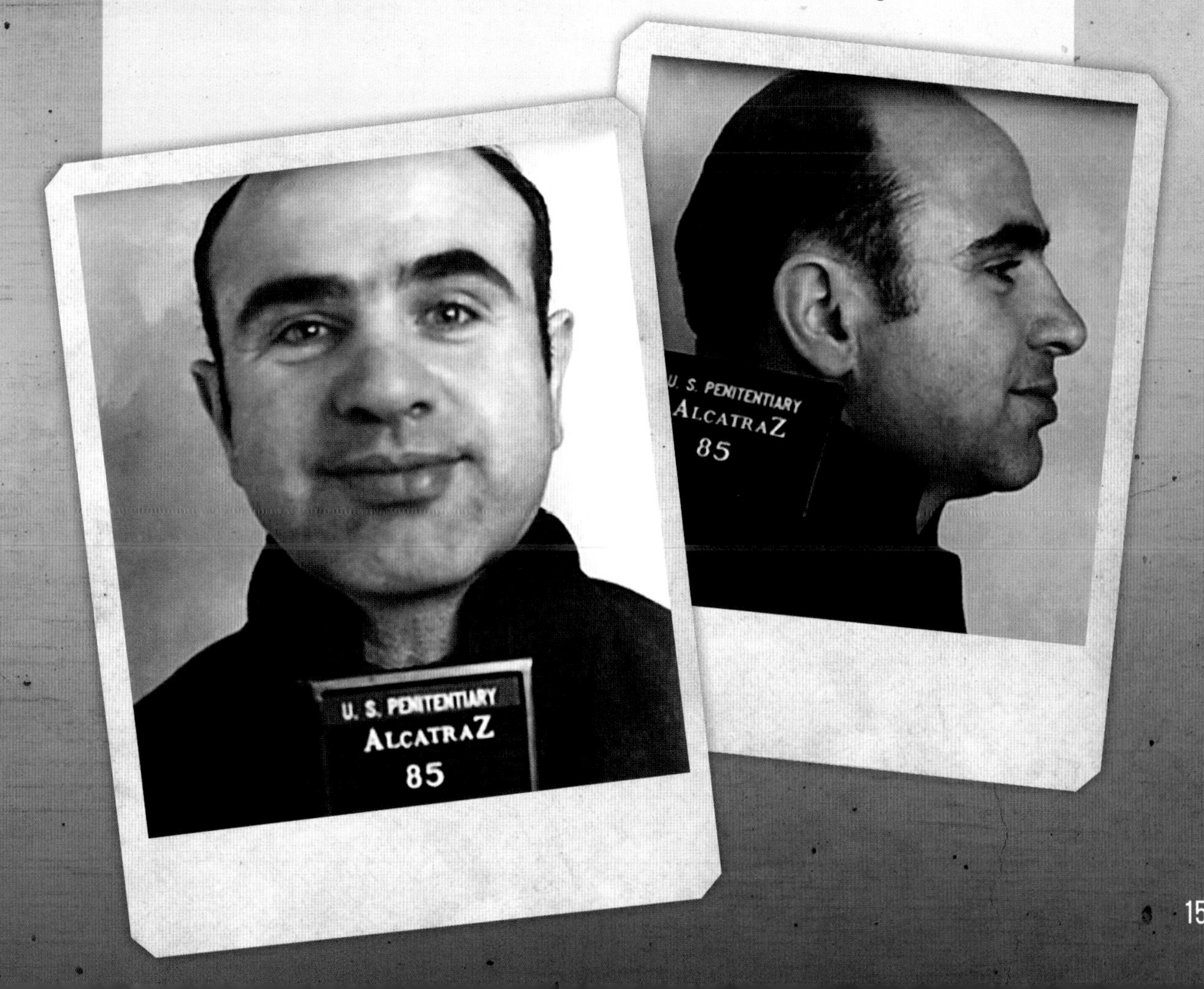

It was against the rules for children to have pretend weapons on Alcatraz, though some did sneak them in. Authorities worried that a guard might mistake a child's toy gun for a real one.

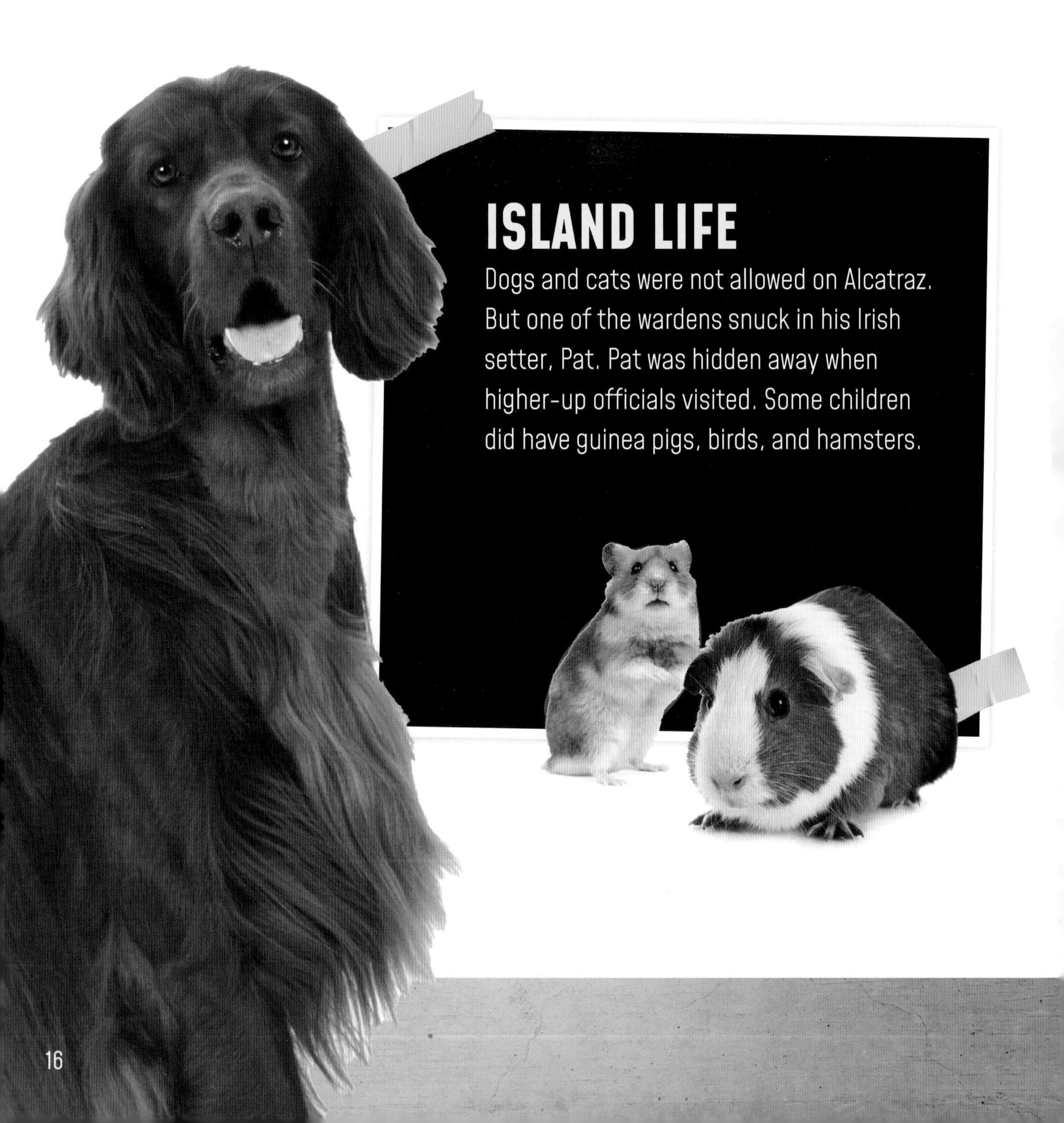

ISLAND LIFE

Dogs and cats were not allowed on Alcatraz. But one of the wardens snuck in his Irish setter, Pat. Pat was hidden away when higher-up officials visited. Some children did have guinea pigs, birds, and hamsters.

Most of the time, Alcatraz was a peaceful and safe place to live. The only times residents felt truly in danger were during escape attempts. Over the life of the prison, this happened 14 times. When it did, a siren warned people to go inside and lock their doors. One infamous incident in 1946 was later called the Battle of Alcatraz. Inmates took over the island for three days. Families were on lockdown inside their apartments. The mothers and children who were in San Francisco at the time were stranded there until it was safe to return. The families later heard the heartbreaking news that two guards and three inmates were killed.

U.S. Marines shot gunfire, mortar, and tear gas at the prison to quell the prisoners during the Battle of Alcatraz.

Chapter 3

AN ISOLATED ISLAND

There's a reason Alcatraz prison was built on an island—it was hard to get off of! For prisoners to escape, getting beyond the heavily guarded prison walls was the easy part. After that, an inmate would still have to swim long distances through icy waters.

But the families on Alcatraz had to come and go. There was no school there. There weren't big stores, doctor's offices, or movie theaters. For these things and more, families had to cross the water to San Francisco.

The view of Alcatraz from San Francisco

The families on Alcatraz had it easier than the inmates. They took a ferry boat across to the mainland. It was their link with the outside world. It brought guards and their families to the city and back.

About 70 kids at one time attended school on the mainland. When the boat whistle blew, they'd run down to the dock and file on board. A woman watched from an apartment balcony to make sure no one was missing. The kids would chat and do last-minute homework during the 12-minute ride. In the city, the younger children walked to school accompanied by an adult.

Alcatraz Escape

The most famous Alcatraz escape attempt was made by Frank Morris and brothers John and Clarence Anglin. They started by digging tunnels, which took several months. When they were ready to escape, they placed dummy heads in their beds and then crawled through the tunnels. In the dark, they floated away on a lifeboat made from raincoats. The men were never officially seen again. Most people assumed they drowned. Some of their family members, however, thought they escaped successfully. One relative swore she saw the Anglins at their mother's funeral dressed as women.

Getting on and off the boat at Alcatraz was scary. There was a gap, and the boat would rise and fall with the swells. A crew member had to swing small children across. The captain always worried they'd drop a child into the water, but they never did. When the ferry was docked at the island, the key was sent up to a tall watchtower by pulley. That way, inmates couldn't take over the boat and use it to escape.

No matter the weather, the ferry made 16 to 20 round trips daily. In really bad conditions, kids were allowed to skip school. If the fog was very thick, families sometimes stood on the eastern tip of the island banging pots and pans to guide the boat back to the dock.

As kids got older, they'd take the boat to the city to meet up with friends or attend school dances. But they had to watch the clock. If they missed the midnight boat, they'd be stuck in the city overnight! When this happened, kids had to find a public pay phone. There they could insert a coin and call a friend to stay with in San Francisco.

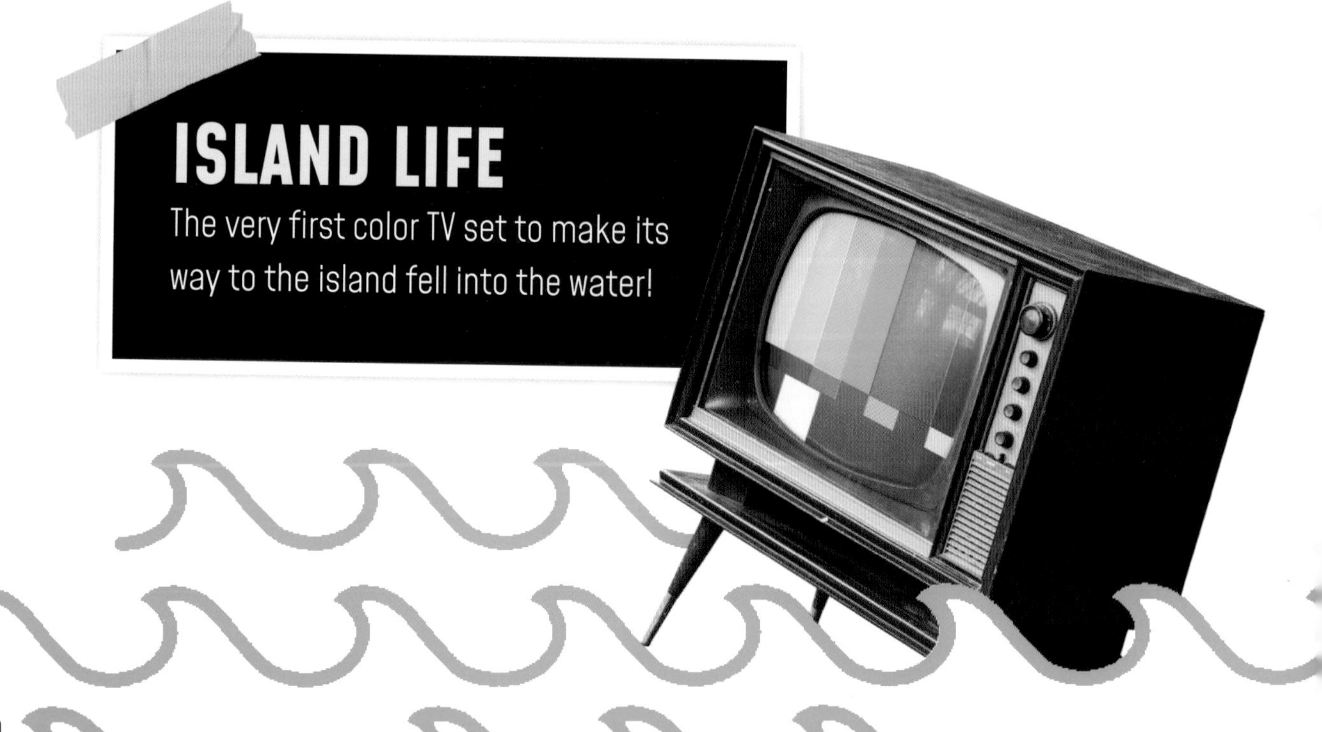

ISLAND LIFE

The very first color TV set to make its way to the island fell into the water!

A guard in a tower above the dock lowered the ferry key down to the guard who drove the boat.

Chapter 4

FUN AND GAMES

Everywhere the kids went on the mainland, people asked, "What's it like to live on Alcatraz?"

The answer? It was fun! The island was a children's playground. Because it was so guarded, parents gave the kids a lot of freedom.

Inmates played handball, baseball, dominoes, chess, and a card game called bridge on their windswept recreation yard. Meanwhile, the children of Alcatraz hung out on the old military parade ground on their side of the island. It was a large concrete yard where soldiers had practiced marching many years before.

The parade ground was perfect for roller-skating and flying kites. Kids also played baseball, touch football, and tennis. Some children developed a clever game for windy days. Two kids on skates would hold a sheet between them as a sail. The wind would blow them clear across the parade ground!

"As boys, we used to explore everywhere around the island. . . . As a kid you tried to get to where you shouldn't be, of course."
– former child resident Chuck Stucker

Kids often climbed on the old, abandoned cannons scattered around the island. The apartment blocks were a good setting for hide-and-seek. Kids fished from the rocks, and teenagers sunbathed there in sunny weather.

Climbing on the cannons was a fun activity for the kids.

To keep employees content, the prison administration provided entertainment. There were social clubs, dance lessons, and dances. In the social hall, there was ping-pong, **billiards**, a bowling alley, and a movie every other week. The inmates got to watch the movie too—but inside the prison.

Not everything was for the kids. At this time, most fathers worked outside the home, and most mothers worked at home, raising children and doing housework. Guards' wives enjoyed a recipe exchange and a sewing circle. They gardened, hosted dinner parties, and organized a talent show. The adults grew as close as the kids.

ISLAND LIFE

In the social hall, kids liked playing music on the jukebox. They could also order a drink at the soda fountain or buy gum from the gumball machine.

A jukebox was a music player that a person could put a coin into and choose a song to play.

Alcatraz Christmas party, 1950

Holidays were extra special on Alcatraz. A favorite event was the end-of-summer watermelon feed. It included games and lots of watermelon. On Halloween, kids trick-or-treated among the apartments. In December, the families lugged Christmas trees over by boat and welcomed Santa. They visited the warden's house for cookies and hot chocolate on Christmas Eve. They also walked around the island singing carols, bringing cheer even to the inmates locked up inside.

"There was a wonderful social life for children. We had numerous parties."
– former child resident Jean Comerford

Chapter 5

THE END OF AN ERA

Alcatraz was two or three times more expensive to run than other prisons. Not only was more staff required, but all water and supplies had to be brought over by boat. In addition, the damp salt air caused the concrete buildings to crumble.

In 1963, word went out that the prison was closing. Sadness spread among the employees and their families. Even the younger kids knew that growing up on Alcatraz was a special experience. Before they left, some of the families took a boat ride around the island. Many people cried.

"As kids it was a phenomenal place to be."
– former child resident Steve Mahoney

Men looked for jobs elsewhere, all across the country. Most found positions at other prisons, but none could compare with life on Alcatraz. Because living there had been such a bonding experience, many of the staff kept in touch. Years later, they organized reunions. At this time, Alcatraz was part of the National Park Service. Some of the children grew up to write books about their extraordinary experiences.

These children weren't the last ones to live on Alcatraz. In 1969, a group of idealistic Native people carried out a peaceful takeover. They called themselves the Indians of All Tribes. An 1868 treaty stated that government land that was not being used went back to the ownership of Native peoples. This group occupied the island for about 18 months. Their goal was to bring attention to the brutal ways in which Native peoples had been treated over the years.

A number of children were part of this important **occupation**. Like the kids before them, they played on the parade ground and abandoned cannons. Unlike the earlier children, these kids got to see inside the prison!

The occupation of Alcatraz ended in 1970. Two years later, the island became part of the Golden Gate National Recreation Area. Today, about 1.5 million people visit every year. They peer into cells and imagine inmates eating in the dining room. To these visitors, Alcatraz seems like a dark, dangerous place. But to the children who once lived there, it was a great place to grow up.

Alcatraz Timeline

1853 The U.S. military begins to develop the barren rocky island of Alcatraz as a fort to guard the city of San Francisco.

1854 Construction of the first lighthouse on the Pacific Coast is completed on Alcatraz.

1861 Alcatraz becomes a military **detention center**.

1861–1934 Military families live on the Island, creating Victorian-style cottage gardens.

1934 Alcatraz becomes a **federal** prison.

1946 The Battle of Alcatraz, the bloodiest escape attempt, leaves three inmates and two guards dead.

1962 The most famous escape takes place. Three inmates float away on a homemade rubber raft. Their bodies are never found.

1963 Too expensive to maintain, Alcatraz prison closes.

1969–70 Native activists occupy Alcatraz to raise awareness about the brutal treatment of Native peoples over the years.

1972 Alcatraz becomes part of the Golden Gate National Recreation Area.

GLOSSARY

billiards (BIL-yurds)—a game in which people use a stick, called a cue, to hit balls around a table

commute (kuh-MYOOT)—to travel to work or school by bus, train, or car

detention center (di-TEN-shuhn SEN-tur)—a place where people suspected of a crime are held

federal (FED-ur-uhl)—relating to the U.S. government

inmate (IN-mayt)—a prisoner

notorious (nuh-TOR-ee-uhss)—being well known for something bad

occupation (ahk-yuh-PAY-shuhn)—when an area of land is taken over and controlled by a different group than the one previously in control

READ MORE

Bruchac, Joseph. *Of All Tribes: American Indians and Alcatraz.* New York: Abrams Books for Young Readers, 2023.

Chandler, Matt. *Daring Escape from Alcatraz.* North Mankato, MN: Capstone Press, an imprint of Capstone, 2022.

Marino, Andy. *Escape from Alcatraz.* New York: Scholastic Inc., 2024.

INTERNET SITES

Federal Bureau of Prisons: The Rock
bop.gov/about/history/alcatraz.jsp

National Park Service: Alcatraz Island
nps.gov/alca/index.htm

The Children That Grew Up on Alcatraz Had a More Fun Childhood Than You Might Imagine
historycollection.com/the-children-that-grew-up-on-alcatraz-had-a-more-fun-childhood-than-you-might-imagine/

INDEX

ABOUT THE AUTHOR

Emma Bland Smith is a librarian and an award-winning author of many books for children (including *The Gardener of Alcatraz*, *How Science Saved the Eiffel Tower*, and *The Fabulous Fannie Farmer: Kitchen Scientist and America's Cook*). She lives in San Francisco in an old creaky house with her family and pets. Visit her online at www.emmabsmith.com.